SHARKS!

PHONICS

Chomp and Chew

Book 3: ch (Beginning blend)

By Quinlan B. Lee

Photo Credits: cover: Dimitri Otis/Getty Images; title page: Luis Javier Sandoval/Getty Images; pages 2-3: Watt Jim/Getty Images; pages 4-5: Dimitri Otis/Getty Images; pages 6-7: Luis Javier Sandoval/Getty Images; page 8: Jim Abernethy/National Geographic; pages10-11: Greg Amptman/Shutterstock; pages12-13: Ingo Schulz/Corbis; page14: Nalu Photo/iStockphoto; page16: Tui De Roy/Minden Pictures.

ISBN 978-0-545-74700-4

12 11 10 9 8 7 6 5 4 3 2 1   14 15 16 17 18/0

Printed in China   145

First Printing, September 2014

SCHOLASTIC INC.

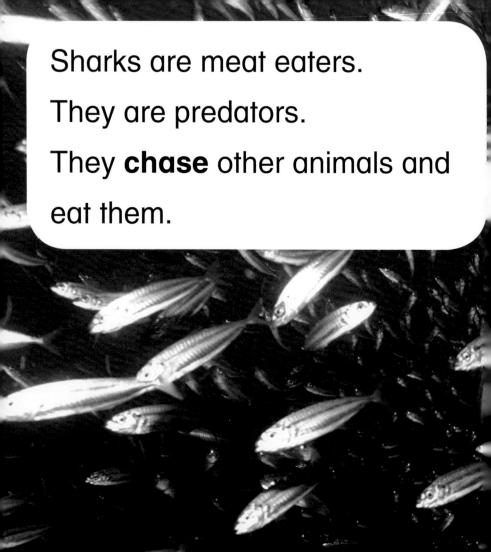

Sharks are meat eaters.

They are predators.

They **chase** other animals and eat them.

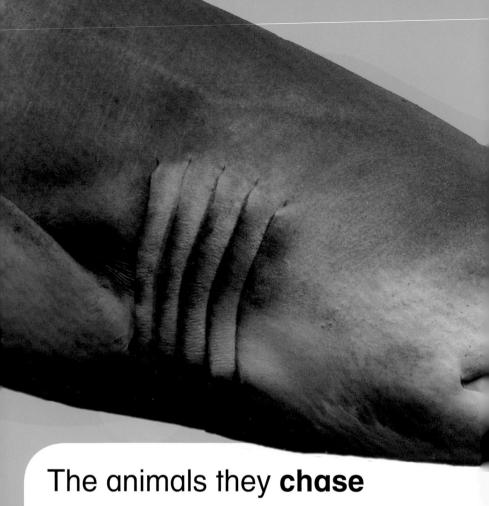

The animals they **chase** are called prey.

Sharks like to **chase** fish, crabs, seals, and even other sharks!

The **chase** is on!

The fish take off.

The shark takes off.

The fish swim left,
then **change** quickly.
The shark **changes**, too.

Finally the shark catches up to the fish.

The shark **charges** the fish.

Check out those teeth!

Chomp!

The shark **chomps** the fish.

It **chews** the fish.

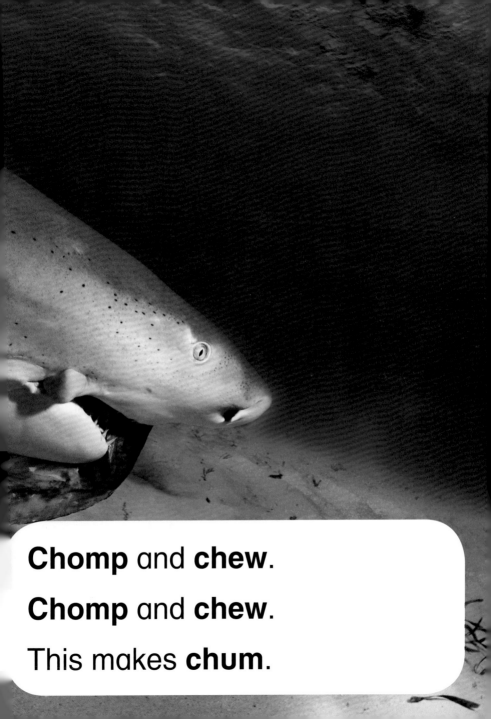

Chomp and **chew**.

Chomp and **chew**.

This makes **chum**.

Chum is **chunks** of fish and blood.

The **chum** brings in more sharks.

When sharks smell **chum**,
they **charge**.
They want **chunks** of fish, too.

It is **chow** time for the sharks!